AMERICAN PORN

Heathcote Williams

‘The old world is dying, and the new world struggles to be born; now is the time of monsters.’

— Antonio Gramsci

First edition Thin Man Press 2017

A CIP catalogue record for this title is available from the British Library.
ISBN 978-0-9930141-8-5
Thin Man Press, London

Contents

Acknowledgments

Grateful acknowledgments to Susan de Muth, John Lahr, Elena Caldera, Colin Gibson, Eddie Mizzi, Rex Pyke, Dave Motion, Lily Williams, Nigel Allen, Graham Yates, Jon Kunac-Tabinor, Carrie Giunta, Paula Finch, Robin Beste, Martin Wilkinson, Simon Drake and Mike Figgis.

Three of these poems were first published in a limited edition of 36 copies by Gerard Bellaart of Cold Turkey Press. A reading by the author of *The United States of Porn*, recorded by Jan Herman, was released by Sea Urchin Editions in 2013.

The United States of Porn

Amerigo Vespucci, of Florence,
A peddler of pornography,
Gave his name to America.

When Martin Waldseemuller,
A sixteenth-century map-maker,
Was looking for a suitable name

For a particular land mass to the West,
Thought to hold a shortcut —
The fabled North West Passage to India —

Long sought after by navigators who hoped
That it might spare them circumventing the Cape
On that continent's treacherous, southernmost tip.

Waldseemuller thought at first of calling it the
        North Indies
(In line with the West Indies and the East Indies),
Until the name of Amerigo Vespucci entered
        his mind.

Amerigo, a senior steward of Lorenzo de Medici,
Had travelled both to Guinea and to Brazil
And written accounts of his adventures

In which he revealed that, after living with
Amazon Indians
For all of two weeks, he had discovered
That his hosts in the rain forest were naked.

This of course was appropriate on their part —
Their being nearer the equator than Florence —
However, Amerigo, their beady-eyed guest, foresaw a
market

In the drawing-rooms of Italy for some prurient tales
In which he'd detail their customs and invent some
more.
With a tabloid glee he'd make out the Indians to be
outlandish —

They frolicked in the sun, had carefree orgies; and
fecklessly killed
Unwanted children, on whom, Amerigo would insist,
they snacked.
In these fables, the indigenous people were
erotomaniac cannibals.

His readers lapped up his exploitational gallimaufry
Set in a paradise untrammelled by Church or State
And his salacious tales became an Italian bestseller.

Even though Amerigo was never in fact to set foot
upon it,
Waldseemuller gave what would become the USA his
name.
It was just business: Waldseemuller was spicing up
his maps

By capitalizing on the notoriety of Amerigo's
accounts.
Thus America, along with its dream, was named
after a porn writer
Who worked for the Medici, the mafia of the Middle
Ages.

'In my beginning is my end,' wrote Eliot in
The Four Quartets
And now Amerigo's bankrupt landmass survives on
pornography
And on the profits from the sale of its instruments of
killing.

Chatsworth, California, is the HQ of America's
Pornocracy
Where the vulnerable are herded by the voracious
Into the maws of a multi-trillion-dollar industry.

An industry strewn with suicides who've lost their
identity
To repetitive humping in exchange for money and for
drugs
In a forlornly unfulfilled wasteland frantic for a hole
to fill.

A new porn video is produced every thirty minutes in
the USA
Where ninety-seven percent of all pornographic web
pages
Are generated for a global food chain of interlinked
Personal Computers.

. . .

When Adolf Hitler was preparing to invade Poland,
The sinister, lip-smacking troll, Doctor Goebbels,
Hobbled beside him, straight out of a Wagner opera.

Goebbels was an expert on how to debilitate
opponents
And, in the case of Poland, he'd make pornography
a weapon
Targeting Polish officers in an erotic PsyWar.

They were infiltrated with pornography by the Nazis
As a matter of state policy... for Goebbels thought
That if they possessed it, they'd put up less of a fight.

Goebbels believed pornography worked as an
anaesthetic –
His enemies, ironically, could be softened by being
stiffened –
And his opponents could be maddened by graphic
portrayals

Of their wives, at home, in the Polish officer
husbands' absence...
Doctor Goebbels knew his Freud and his Bernays
and his Adler
And how psychosexual mechanisms worked.

Still more is known now through hooking up lab rats
To electrodes that stimulate the pleasure centre of
the brain;
If they're placed in a cage with two buttons to press,

One dispensing food, the other dispensing
orgasms,
Typically, the rats will soon starve themselves to
death
If they haven't already died from exhaustion.

Goebbels knew sexual stimulation to be a powerful
method
Of social control and that's why its manipulations
are still rated,
Given its soporific effect on consumerism's
lab rats —

Particularly handy in a pre-revolutionary situation
Where levels of inequality exist such as never seen
before.
Pornography is capitalism's reward for political
apathy.

Pornography is the sensual soma of
Brave New World
The insidious tranquillizer that neuters collective
action
So that, in the US, few are angered by just fifty
people

Having more wealth than half of America's remaining
citizens put together,
And few are provoked by another hundred and fifty
new billionaires
Joining the American billionaire club every year,

While twenty million people die from hunger and
disease
And while the average billionaire annually spends
twenty-five million dollars
On food, entertainment, then more food and
entertainment,

Enough to feed seventy thousand hungry people for a
year.
Imperial Rome spent fifteen percent of its tax revenue
on its war machine,
The imperial USA spends fifty-four percent of its tax
revenue on its war machine.

Or rather on Defence Contractors — the body guards of
an elite —
Because the more money that corporate America
hoards,
The more weapons it needs to protect itself...

To protect itself from the consequences of its own
actions.
Amerigo's country is founded on the genocide of its
First Nations
And sustained by genocide in countries all over the
world.

Amerigo's country has sponsored serial holocausts
In Central and South East Asia, and the Middle East,
All with the same motive: capturing another country's
resources.

Forty-six percent of children who lose an arm or leg in
the world,
Lose it to a weapon manufactured by an American
company.
The US government receives $2,650 billion in taxes
each year,

Of which fifty-four percent goes towards war and
destruction.
'We are bankers. You are nothing, and when our greed
Gets the better of us, you must help us out.'

The sex toy industry is valued at $15 billion;
It's enough to provide for the healthcare needs of all
women
In impoverished countries. But, 'We are American
bankers,

'We invest in sex toys. They have a high yield. You are
nothing.
'We are American bankers. We are happiest if we're
making money;

‘Making money by people pleasuring themselves with
machines.’

As befits a country named after the Medici mafia’s
gopher,
America spends more money on weapons each year
Than the whole world spends on food and drinks.

In 1998, Lockheed Martin refused to give free prosthetic
limbs
To children maimed by its weapons.
‘We are American bankers. We invest in weapons. You
are nothing.

‘We are citizens of the United States of Porn.
‘We live in an armed Imperialist pornocracy.
‘We are kleptomaniac bankers, you are nothing.’

‘A few thousand miles of cannibal land’ was how
Robert Korner, CIA Adviser
To John F Kennedy, described resource-rich
West Papua before both
Backed an invasion to the benefit of the US Mining
company Freeport.

The same allegations of cannibalism as Amerigo Vespucci
once made

Allowed the Papuans to be slaughtered by the
American Empire –
To be treated as unpeople and therefore ripe for
Exploitation…

Whilst back in the USA, in the cradle of another
civilization,
Porn barons bewitch tame porn tribes to act out
primitive rituals:
Smeared with baby oil and wearing rubber sheathes,
they eat each other.

There are twenty-two million women in the world who
spend five hours a day
Collecting water for their children and families.
During the financial crisis there were American bankers

In Wall Street who watched porn for up to five hours a
day.
But a marriage between such unfeeling profiteers from
poverty
And porn addicts is an ideal marriage since both are
bankers

And porn addicts distort the way you love your fellow
man.
'We are bankers, we crunch numbers. You are nothing,

'We are bankers, you are nothing. Pass the Kleenex.'

Bigger than Hollywood, porn pump-starts the US
economy —
The cream-filling in its military-industrial sandwich
Upon which the rest of the world is now force-fed.

Every second in Amerigo-Vespucci-land thousands of
dollars
Are spent on porn by two hundred and fifty million
citizens
Who look away from their porn screens

And wave wet tissues at their Statue of Liberty
Then smile, slack-jawed, 'Look Mom, look at what we
can do.'
Then it's back to the screen: porn screens in the White
House;

Porn screens in the Pentagon; porn screens in the
Supreme Court;
Porn screens in the Senate offices; porn screens in
Congress.
Two hundred and fifty million militarized masturbators

Are enslaved by billionaire pornocrats relentlessly
promoting

Cybernetic snake-pits of squirming bodies, all gasping,
'Ah!'
'Ah!' 'Ah!' 'Ah!' 'Ah!' 'Ah!' 'Ah!' 'Ah!' 'Ah!' 'Ah!' 'Ah!' 'Ah!'
'Ah!'

While all are in denial: 'I don't like cocaine, I just like
the smell of it'.
'It's got nothing to do with sexual belligerence, it's
harmless.
'If people want to see people holding women down.
So what?'

Romantic arousal is now mediated by favourite porn
clips;
One addict confessed to logging on to three hundred
vaginas
Before getting up in the morning — indicative of synaptic
change.

'What pornography is really about, ultimately, isn't sex
but death,'
Said Susan Sontag, and she was echoed by J G Ballard:
'A widespread taste for pornography means that nature

'Is alerting us to some threat of extinction.'
'When liberty comes,' said Wilde, 'with hands dabbled
in blood

‘It is hard to shake hands with her.’ Equally hard to
shake hands

With those panting and throbbing due to repetitive
stress disorder
Induced by Miss Porn USA and her all-enveloping porn
cloud that governs
Global weather, despite pornography being as dull as
golf.

In the caves of Lascaux, prehistoric man drew virile
penises on stick figures
But they may not have rooted him to the spot while he
pleasured himself
For instead he’d leave the darkness of the cave to
pursue his own history –

Being sensible enough to know that compulsively
playing with himself -
Preying on his own energy and milking himself for
hours on end
While watching flickering images - might make him
prone to predators.

Amerigo Vespucci, of Florence, a peddler of pornography,
Set his seal on America: trillions in debt; its economy
sexualized;

Stealing others' resources at gunpoint, and unable to
feed itself.

'They are living like parasites off the global economy,'
Vladimir Putin said of America, which now only lacks
William S. Burroughs[i],
Former pest control expert, to describe her final death-
orgasm.

Health Warning

Health warning:
Saturation Coverage
Of the US Election
Can cause brain damage.

For nine months
US Supremacism
Indulges itself
In an election
For the US President.

Somehow or other
This always involves
The US electorate
Watching candidates
Spending billions
On trying to persuade it
To elect murderers.

Only the religious slaves
Of a militarized state
Will be elected.
No applications
From pacifists or humanists
Will be entertained.

Four million homeless
Have no representative.
It's mass murderers
Who are elected
To rule the richest country
In the entire world.

Support for this farce
Comes from people believing
That America
Sets an example
To the world's democracies
And should therefore have
Mass media coverage
Non-stop, twenty-four seven...

It's relentless.
Male or female; black or white
It will be a mass murderer
Who is elected.
The moral high ground
Is laid claim to by the world's policeman
As the mass-murdering begins.

In the US election,
A corporate dictatorship promotes
Its Presidential toy

And the President's wealth
Is increased by his term of office —
Otherwise, no change.
No one has vision.
It being beyond their Presidential imaginings
To think of a world beyond war.

Trump versus Clinton

November 2016

The total obscenity of the American Dream
Comes to fruition in Donald John Trump:
'We need a leader that wrote *The Art of the Deal,*'
He declared, on his Presidential stump.

What's wrong is that Trump's best-selling volume,
On the virtues of property speculation,
Wasn't written by him but by one Tony Schwarz
(Now dreading Trump as leader of his nation).

The Art of the Deal established Donald J. Trump
As the archetypal successful tycoon.
Schwarz presented him in the best possible light –
Striving to hide a poisonous buffoon.

'I put lipstick on a pig,' Schwarz later would say
When overcome with remorse,
For he'd branded Trump as a winning charmer –
One that an electorate could endorse.

Whereas, in his Presidential run-up, 'the Donald'
Would soon reveal his true colours:
'It really doesn't matter what the media write',
Trump says,

'As long as you've got a young piece of ass.'

Despite self-enchanted claims to be a self-made man
Trump's wealth has been largely inherited
From father Fred, a slum landlord and speculator,
Who was once notoriously prosecuted

By the US Justice Department for refusing
To rent to African-Americans –
To do so clashed with the beliefs Fred gleaned
From his attendance at Klu Klux Klan rallies[ii].

It's said that the apple doesn't fall far from the tree
And so the son is true to Fred's prejudice
With Donald's plans to exclude Mexicans with a wall
And to make Mexico pay for the privilege.

Trump's first wife, Ivana, famously claimed
That Trump was a fan of Adolf Hitler
And that he kept a copy of Hitler's speeches,
My New Order, in his bedside cabinet.

'The beauty of me is that I'm very rich,' says the gilded
toad.
'The point is, you can never be too greedy.
'My IQ is one of the highest - and you all know it!'
He then changes gear to become simply creepy:

'I've said if Ivanka weren't my daughter,
'Perhaps I would be dating her.'
If he can sink to using incest as a come-on to gain
the White House
What's to stop such a pervert killing her or perhaps
eating her?

When the publisher Random House gave him an
advance
Of half a million to write his autobiography,
They sent a mock-up to Trump Towers for his
approval –
They'd not held back on the typography:

They'd featured his name, TRUMP, in gold block
capitals
With him being depicted as a new Alexander the Great.
'Please make my name much bigger,' responded the
man
Whose vampirish megalomania was his favourite trait.

Schwarz saw Trump as driven by an insatiable hunger
For 'money, praise, and celebrity.'
He described him by saying, 'He's a living black hole!'
And he viewed his mindset with hilarity.

Trump would proclaim that an apartment

In one of his latest developments
Has been sold to a Prince or a Sultan
To add kudos to his establishment.

'Prince Charles has bought several,' he'd insist
Although there wasn't a shred of evidence,
But snobs and New York sheep fell for his ploy
And Trump gained his golden recompense.

This mega-vulgarian who blows his own trumpet
So hard you think he's likely to blow a fuse –
This red-faced Aryan with his combed-over hair
Is a charlatan whose every game-plan is a ruse.

He has three thousand five hundred lawsuits pending[iii];
He takes rides on the 'Lolita Express'
To a Caribbean island filled with underage girls
Thanks to Jeffrey Epstein, a slave to excess –

A convicted sex criminal, friends with Prince Andrew,
Bill Clinton, and other over-privileged sleazeballs.
Trump joined him as a sex-tourist and an orgy-goer
With a penchant for raping thirteen-year-old girls.

One alleged victim, not named in Court documents,
Claims that during one 'savage sexual attack'

Trump tied her to a bed, then ‘proceeded to forcibly
rape’ her
While she ‘loudly pleaded’ for him to stop.

The billionaire is alleged to have ‘screamed that he would
do whatever he wanted,’
Struck her with his open hands then threatened
the girl:
‘Were she ever to reveal any of the details of the sexual
abuse,
‘She and her family would be “physically harmed if not
Killed”[iv].’

At the age of 22, Trump had four military deferments
To get out of fighting in Vietnam.
He claimed he’d had an ‘uncomfortable bone’ in one his
feet
Yet couldn’t remember which foot caused the ‘problem’.

That his millionaire father was instrumental in this
great patriot
Avoiding Vietnam was also the truth –
Leaving Trump to say flippantly that his ‘personal
Vietnam’
Was to have avoided sexual diseases in his youth.

Trump's buildings are erected by craftsmen whose bills
he often ignores.
His Trump University peddles Mickey Mouse degrees.
Here's a man who declares war on 'political correctness'
As it stops him from abusing whomsoever he pleases.

Foul-tempered and violent he singles out hecklers
To be beaten up or pepper-sprayed by bodyguards.
'I'd like to punch him in the face,' he says of a protester,
This Neanderthal, and virulently racist blow-hard.

Now imagine Donald Trump in the White House,
Conjuring his self-serving lies out of thin air.
With his sleek little fingers fondling the nuclear codes,
The demagogue grins and mutters, 'Do I dare?'

'It's freezing and snowing in New York – we need global
warming!'
Is Trump's take on an apocalyptic predicament.
'It's impossible to keep him focused on any topic,' says
Schwarz,
'Other than his own self-aggrandizement.'

'All Moslems should leave the United States now,'
Says Trump on a populist roll.
The US father of a Muslim soldier killed in action
Condemns Trump as 'a black soul.'

It's claimed by former MI6 agent, Chris Steele –
Who heard it from the Russian FSB –
That Donald Trump likes to pay prostitutes
To shower him with golden pee.

A recording was made in Moscow's Ritz-Carlton
Of the future President's urophiliac peaks –
Blissfully unaware while bathing in hookers' widdle,
He was giving new meaning to Wikileaks.

Killary

Donald Trump's warmongering ex-rival is little better –
A humourless Iron Lady in hock to Wall Street:
Who crows after Gaddafi's murder by CIA stooges:
Sadistically gloating, 'We came; we saw; he died!'.

Secretary Hillary Clinton's emails show that Libya's
plan
To create a gold-backed African currency to compete
With the dollar was the real motive for NATO
intervention,
And Hillary's death squad saw to it that the job
was complete[v].

Hillary's role in the bombing of Libya
As the US Secretary of State

Led to a body-count of over twelve thousand
And to the ISIS[vi] regime of hate.

Clinton leaves a trail of more bloody coups:
Both in Honduras and in the Ukraine.
Appropriately, nine out of ten US arms makers
Are generously funding her campaign.

Despite 400,000 civilians being killed in Syria
This neo-con Mother Kali calls for more.
Unable to mind her own business, she demands
'Regime change'... which is code for war.

Hillary Clinton's support for Jihadists in Syria
Would further fuel the Islamic State –
Now with powerful US weapons and equipment
With which to revive its Caliphate.

She has armed Saudis with sophisticated weapons
To carry out genocide in Yemen.
'The nuclear option should not be off the table,'
She has said in relation to Iran.

Bill and Hillary's private slush fund,
The Clinton Global Foundation,
Gives less than ten percent to charity
Despite its declared intentions[vii].

The Clinton Foundation exists to open the door
To the third world's valuable resources:
If corporate interests donate to its crooked coffers
Then the Clintons will pressurize world leaders.

If these are the best candidates that are on offer
In the American Petri dish of democratic depravity,
Then maybe it's time for the system to crumble
And to be replaced by non-violent anarchy.

It's sick to have billionaires or their puppets
Controlling the future of the species.
American democracy doesn't count as democracy
But as a notifiable disease.

President Donald J. Trump

World Emperor

'Donald Trump looks like someone playing a President in a porno.'

– Frankie Boyle, *America Autopsy*, BBC 2

'I don't like to analyze myself because I might not like what I see.'

– Donald Trump

On buying a beauty spot in Scotland for a golf-course
And for luxury condominiums,
Trump notices some old houses on the horizon
And he orders them bulldozed to oblivion.

On seeing a woman that he desires, he oafishly
Recommends 'grabbing her pussy'.
He boasts that, 'My fame lets me take liberties;
'My fame allows me to abuse her.'

Trump's grandfather ran brothels in the Yukon
And to his grandson, also, people are for sale.
Trump's ego tells him he has supernatural powers
And that almost nothing is beyond the pale.

'I will deport twelve million Latinos', Donald insists –
This buddy of asset strippers and union busters –
A charlatan who papers over his character's cracks
With bank loans and with megalomaniac bluster.

Trump was a casino owner (a synonym for gangster),
A suitable past for the President of casino capitalism
Who boasts about who he's been able to shake down,
And who represents a homegrown neo-fascism.

Trump's a demagogue who's prone to magical thinking
With a compulsion to build concrete penises
Upon which his name appears in enormous letters
And whose robotic staff repeat, 'he's a genius.'

He has pretended to be anti-establishment
And to be standing up for the little guy,
Yet without Wall Street and the Deutsche Bank
This exhibitionist parasite would die.

He's a slave to his monumental indebtedness.
He owes six hundred million dollars.
But now that he's President he can pay his creditors,
The mob and their sinister callers –

While doubtless remaining reluctant to pay taxes
For he regards tax evasion as an art.

When he's challenged about not filing tax returns
He brags, 'That makes me smart[viii].'

He's risen to power on the magniloquent claim
That he'll make America great,
While representing the lowest common denominator
Of his country's racist hate.

In 1992 Casino Control fined him $200,000
For removing African-American card dealers
From his Plaza Hotel's casino to appease the racism
Of the Plaza's big-spending gamblers.

Trump would disparage his black employees as
'lazy'.
'I've got black accountants and isn't it funny?' He'd say,
'Black guys counting my money! I hate it. The only kind
of people
'I want are short guys that wear yarmulkes every day[ix].'

'When Donald and Ivana came to the casino,'
Recalls Kip Brown, an employee at Trump's Castle,
'The bosses would order all the black people off the
floor,'
He told the *New Yorker* in a 2015 article[x].

Regarding an African-American President

As an affront to his sensibility,
Trump became vocal in the 'Birther' movement
Questioning Obama's legitimacy.

Trump failed to disavow the Ku Klux Klan
When they supported his candidacy;
He'd airily pretend he didn't know who they were
With an ignorance approaching lunacy.

Donald J. Trump has been elected President
Of the US's plutocratic pornocracy –
A plot twist, and suddenly the whole world
Is having to adjust to his squalid reality.

He believes women should suffer punishment
If they decide to have abortions.
He sees life as conquest and victory and winning,
As if in a childish competition.

In a half-hearted apology for mocking women's looks
Trump says he does it 'to be entertaining' —
Unaware that he himself is overweight and bright
orange
And hardly qualifies as an oil painting.

'I'd bring back a hell of a lot worse than waterboarding,'
Says Trump who advocates torture.

'When I say they'll do as I tell them, they'll do as I tell
them[xi],'
Is how he plans to overcome any legal stricture.

Fifty billion tons of carbon dioxide a year are pumped
Into the atmosphere, causing deadly climate change,
Yet Trump says he'll cancel the planet-saving treaties
The international community has arranged.

Despite the polar ice-caps melting and sea levels
rising,
He defies the science on global warming shamelessly
By putting Myron Ebell, a climate-change denier, paid
by Exxon Mobil,
In charge of the Environmental Protection Agency[xii].

So more earthquakes are certain to happen,
And extreme heat will now be inevitable.
One man's hot air will have consequences
As air becomes less and less breathable.

'We need some global warming. It's freezing!'
Trump would joke while he was out campaigning
Then America's Emperor repeats his strident rhetoric
And his insistence that 'the swamp needs draining.'

When planning permission for Trump towers in
Argentina was withheld,
The President Elect was displeased;
A call from Argentine Premier Mauricio Marci
Was used to urge that planning regulations be eased.

Trump using his office to promote Trump business,
His loose talk of nuclear weapons, make audiences
shiver.
Before Donald J. Trump has even been inaugurated
He's the most corrupt and dangerous President ever.

He may also be the nastiest.
He built a wall to block certain Scottish residents' view
of the sea,
As revenge on those who campaigned against his golf
course.
He sent them a bill. They refused to pay.

'Be polite, but have a plan to kill everybody you meet.'
Are the paranoid words of General 'Mad Dog' Mattis
Which have so impressed President Donald J. Trump,
That he's made this mad dog top dog, Secretary of Defence.

He threatens to attack ISIS with nuclear weapons —
To use a nuclear sledgehammer to crack a nut —

Unable to see that every Trump Tower would be
Transformed into a radioactive mud hut.

Donald Trump is really Donald Drumpf,
To give him his ancestral, and risible name.
It suggests dumbness, even the passing of wind...
As well as the merciful transience of fame.

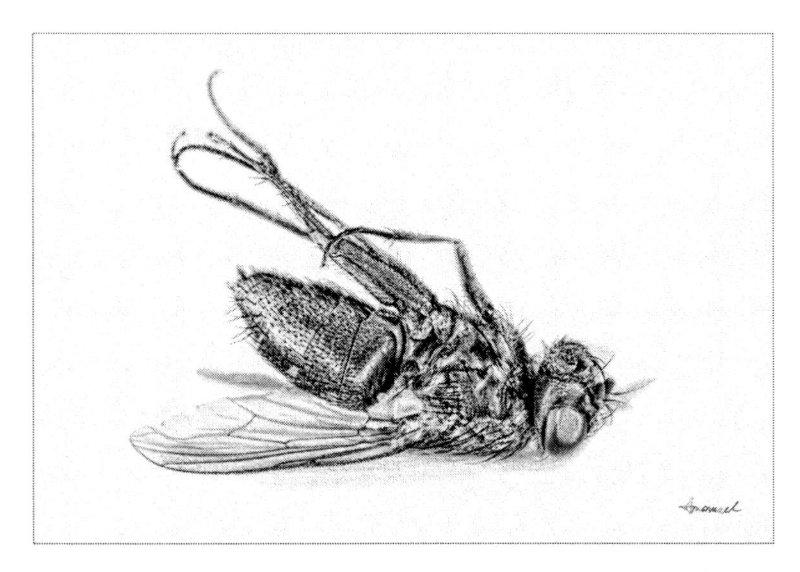

Image via Imgur

'Swatting the hapless insect on the back of his hand

and shaking the corpse to the floor'

The White House Fly

While the White House is seething with Secret Service
special agents,
And weighed down by weapons protecting America's
Holy of Holies,
And as racks of ground-to-air Stinger missiles
invigilate its no-fly zone,
An uninvited renegade breaches the saturation
surveillance.

On a warm June day in the East Room of the
White House,
During a keynote interview with incoming President,
Barack Obama,
Expressly set up so he can 'assess his current media
standing',
A sprightly fly penetrates all the armour-plated
security.

A glistening Harlequin, intricately miniaturized —
The anarchic Don Juan of the natural world —
It pirouettes on a sunbeam, speed-dances in mid-air,
Seeking out sweetness to fuel its serenades.

It ascends and descends; skips, zooms and capers
And deftly defies the earth's gravitational pull;

Then, with its compound eye, it negotiates its way
Past bulky figures and CNBC's bright lights[xiii].

'Hey! Get outta here!' America's 44th President snaps
fretfully;
Addressing 'the signature characteristic of our
Admin- '
He's forced to interrupt himself in the middle of a
lengthy sentence,
Distracted by the signature buzz of this summer fly.

Anxiously aware of the incoming President's
impatient irritation,
And house-trained to turn trivia into historical
events,
His earnest interviewer, John Harwood, declares
obsequiously,
'That's the most persistent fly I've ever seen.'

Regarding the interviewer's remark as a call to arms,
the President strikes,
Swatting the hapless insect on the back of his hand
and shaking the corpse to the floor.
'That was pretty impressive, wasn't it?', The President
invites approval

Before exploding victoriously, 'I got the sucker!'
At which the room swells with 'Jesus!' and ardent
gasps of 'Nice!'
As all vie to outdo each other with coos of
admiration.

'You want to film that? It's right there. There it is!',
the President excitedly urges.
He indicates his fallen victim as he lets out a
fastidious 'Yegh!'
And the camera crew focus on the trembling speck
on the East Room carpet
For the world to share in the President's triumphant
victory.

Still milking the moment, he alerts his Press
Secretary, 'Did you see that, Gibbs?'.
Gibbs beetles off to ensure that the fly's death-throes
are framed in the most flattering light:
In a voiceover he name-checks the Karate Kid who
caught flies with chopsticks
(Though not telling viewers that the Kid's cachet
derived from letting them go).

After America's new Caesar gives the thumbs-down
to a belittled fly
The victory goes viral on global news media

With television's Coliseum baying, 'Go for it, Mr
President!'
And 'All flies are evil!'; the commentariat scorns
other ways to evict them
For isn't every President issued with a Free Pass to
kill?

Yet no one queries the fly's 'bad-guy' stereotype or
wonders if it's misplaced...
For, as well as breaking down waste to generate
topsoil for man's survival,
Life would be buried under piles of bodies and
beneath organic matter
Were it not for the purposeful existence of the President's
present quarry, clearing man's path.

But, 'Shoot first, ask questions afterwards' is the
national characteristic;
Though without flies, stomachs would be half-full
and spring would fall silent,
With plants from catnip to chocolate-yielding cocoa
withering up and dying,
Since flies pollinate... so killing one to show off
comes close to self-harm.

Though the Blue Bottle and the Green Bottle aren't
the greatest respecters of persons

Each fly's agenda matters as much as any human's,
even a VIP,
For while it seeks out plant nectar, it performs
symbiotic tasks, just like a bee,
It services most edible crops: onion, carrot, sesame...
even coffee and tea.

Less temperamental than other pollinators, and less
subject to disease,
Flies are crucial to the life-cycle of lettuce, broccoli,
radish, avocado...
They've a starring role in the growth of cabbage,
peppers, and garlic;
Without flies, no sunflowers, their seeds spiralling in
golden ratios — nature's universal pattern.

The insect is life's cornerstone. Break it, the building
crumbles.
Yet they're despised, for man hates nothing more
than those whom he wrongs.

The fly has mastered the art of living together,
thanks to its altruistic social evolution,
And might observe man with some curiosity —
trapped below in his concrete mazes;
Fouling his global nest; incapable of flying without
crashing and combusting.

Flies stare at him serenely then rub their forelegs, as
if in supplication.

For in his concrete colonies, man competes for what he
can't accept he holds in common
And instead, ruins rivals and their shared resources
with self-serving greed;
Deadening his co-operative instincts, he submits to the
corporate rule of puppet kings:
The hood-ornaments with which he decorates the
state-machine he can't drive.

It's a machine that reveals its character by its dire jargon:
'compressing the Kill Chain'...
And the Pentagon now spends a hundred billion dollars to
secure dominion
Though, by a quirky irony, when its Empire-building
soldiers' wounds get infected
The best cleansing agent is a fly, whose maggots consume
their gangrenous pus.

But, of course, if an inconsequential fly makes you gag with
queasy disgust
Then why not just kill it? — though, like the Brave Little
Tailor
In *Grimm's Fairy Tales* who boasted that he had killed
'seven at one blow!'

Whoever does so, risks the invitation, 'Now why stop
at flies?'.

'The snuff aspect of it, killing the fly, was psychologically
useful for Obama...
'He decided to take it out, and he did take it out.'
The President's interviewer, John Harwood, later told
The New York Times –
Meaning that a violent reaction was the favoured default
position.

The Empire's 44th President had been clear, 'We'll lead by
building a 21st century military...
'We'll have the strongest armed forces in the history
of the world.'
And State fear-mongering pumped money into its military
personnel,
Two-million men strong; and then into the makers of
death-toys
like Raytheon; Boeing; General Dynamics and
Schmidt;

And into the electronic warrens of Silicon Valley,
where the wired generation
Serves the CIA, the DIA and the NSA – the
sulphurous acronyms of repression –

Upon which US citizens spend most of their tax dollars and
sponsor atrocities...
For it's war that drives the US economy, and not the
brotherhood of man.
War's Viagra increases the US economy by sixty percent.

On January 23rd, 2009, Obama gave orders
For the dispatch of robotic flies —
Flying drones befouling the countryside in a vengeful
resource war,
Ordered to lay their burning eggs over the Afghan
landscape and the Swat valley in Pakistan.

They interrupt conversations. They interrupt the
whole social fabric.
They interrupt lives altogether.
And then, with their artificial compound eyes, to spy
upon those below,
America's Unmanned Aerial Vehicles hover above
Afghan and Pakistani villages,
Before triggering Hellfire missiles, swatting villagers
dead.

The Predator drone's thermobaric weapons, their
fuel-air explosives,
Work by spreading an incendiary mist which then
ignites.

A vacuum's made by a firestorm tearing apart those
in target buildings
And bursting the internal organs of farmers in
nearby fields.

Mohammed Yaqoob, a Miranshah teacher, reported
that, 'The children are so frightened of drones
'They can't concentrate on their lessons. They just sit
in the classroom
'Looking up at the sky where drones continuously
hover over the town.
'They don't sleep at night. They're afraid of being
bombed in their beds.'

Meanwhile, War Incorporated requires assistance in
spinning its atrocities.
Public Relations company, the Rendon Group, helps
screen embedded reporters
So military excess can be repackaged as 'successful surges',
and innocent farmers as 'terrorists';
To ensure that America's war crimes are seen through a
rose-tinted corporate media.

And the Pentagon spends $4.7 billion on such public
relations:
On what is known as 'information dominance'

Whereby its 'information warriors' neuter all negative
images
And sprinkle war crimes with their *eau de cologne.*

The American public is urged to take an interest in its
military and, in March 2009,
At Creech Air Base's 'Appreciation Day' there was a
'click-and-kill-show'
For taxpayers to study their distant enemies, like
insects on a pane, before execution —
Thanks to drone operators showing off their deadly
game skills for real.

The air ace who once 'slipped the surly bonds of Earth to
touch the face of God'
Is now downgraded by the Pentagon's techno-Taliban
To being a fake flyboy whose 'situational awareness'
derives merely from hours spent gaming
In American arcades, rather than exploring the 'wild
blue yonder'.

An Air Force pilot now need only be someone trained to sit
upright, and who's mastered Gameboy 2;
Flight-Sim avionics ensure that the robot's take-off
and landing is fully automated.
To the Commanders-in-Chief, the drone warlords
zealously directing their squadrons

Of couch potato killers, the Air Force amounts to no
more than a Chair Force,
Burning Afghan children and their colourful kites
with joysticks.

Predator pilots pretend to be heroes from comic
books, vaporizing 'alien forces of doom',
Persuaded that they possess superhuman courage
with just a screen and a knob.
Elated drone operators yell out 'Crispy critters!' on
turning electronic outlines to blackened ashes
Programmed to think of as inferior, people whom
they can now never know,

Corporal, Rick Reyes of the Marine Corps, would tell
Congress in April 2010,
'Almost a hundred per cent of suspected terrorists
turn out to be innocent civilians';
But the airborne murders did not stop.
Impassioned crowds appear in Islamabad holding up
banners:

'STOP DRACULEAN DRONE ATTACKS',
'END THE BLOODSHED OF INNOCENT PAKISTANIS'.
Witnesses described being buzzed by delta-shaped
metal flies terrorizing their communities;

Mechanical fangs spitting explosive projectiles, burning
their flesh and ending their lives.

At distant bases in Nevada, Predator and Raptor drone
pilots with assistant 'sensor operators'
Sit in a screen-filled office; from here they peep at a
colourful, fluttering procession
That moves from the bride's house to the groom's...
From here they might hear people singing
The Pashto wedding song, *'Ahesta boro, Mah-e-man'*,
'Go slowly, my lovely moon.'
But the group at dusk carrying strange instruments
signals 'Red Alert'.

The Pashtun wedding dance, the Attan, once
Athenian and before that Zoroastrian,
Has Pashtun men and women spinning round a fire,
attaining communion;
But at this wedding, in Farah, it would be a dance of
death, finished by swivel seated killers
Swigging sodas and chomping burgers as they send
in their gate-crashing missiles.

The wedding song is overdubbed by US explosives;
The wedding's future offspring killed by a keystroke.

Then, ending their shift, the drone operators use the
drive home to Las Vegas to 'decompress' –
A ritual in which those battle-hardened by swivelling
their Playstation joysticks
Reassure doubtful novices: 'Rag heads incubate terror.
'Zapping 'em saves US lives. Gotta be a neat plus, dude.'

A drone survivor in Granai described an aircraft with no
pilot that had made a '*zzzz zzzz* sound like a fly',
And then he added, 'The bomb's left people sick. Their
mouths bleed when they eat their food.'
He asked, 'The bomb the Americans used in this place;
maybe it's not been used before?'.
But it has; and it contains Depleted Uranium to
cause the same damage to those yet unborn.

Nicknamed 'termites with thermite' by their developers
and funded by the White House,
Micro-drones, like napalm bats, can now enter buildings
and spatter the inhabitants –
They're programmed to find flesh and to burn it with
inextinguishable, chemical flames.
Next to the techno-trolls devising such things, surely
a housefly has soul.

For turning war into an electronic tournament detaches it
from all human emotion;
And recruiting ads for the military now claim, 'The
frontlines are unmanned'
Since, thanks to PlayStation warfare, spilling blood is only
the enemy's problem:
War's murder can now be morally neutral, just the
technophile's eye-candy.

At Army Recruitment Centres, war is now presented
as 'war-gaming'
Where teenagers are handed out model M-16s
To target Computer-Generated Muslims, or round up
'Mexican migrants' at the Border,
And to simulate shooting each of them in the head.

Such games condition a child's eyes, hands and
nervous system
To shoot fast without leaving a moment for reflective
thought —
Then, when their electronic fidgeting has erased
enough computer graphics,
They can be signed up to cause real deaths on army
screens.

'Kill not the moth nor butterfly', said William Blake,
'For the Last Judgment draweth nigh'.

Yet each President's persuaded they're as great as a God,
For they dish out last judgments every day.

Keats would glimpse flies in musk-roses... 'the
 murmurous haunt of flies on summer eves';
And Proust thought of them as the chamber music of
 summer promising new summers of the soul;
Sweet, sad John Clare was consoled by their antics,
 thinking them things of the mind 'like fairies';
And Wordsworth loved the creature's 'tuneful hum',
While Blake modestly saw himself as just a 'happy fly'.

Kit Smart's 'Cat Jeoffrey' would chase and play with a fly
 till all three of them were
Buzzing and humming with electric joy, cavorting
 with a seasoned acrobat
dancing upside down on glass; an exotic stranger
 with honeycomb eyes
And two thousand lenses and no need to be scapegoated
By anyone who can't see that a fly flags up the life of
 the day and deserves to be left alone.

Was there a Pashtun Rumi amongst those whom the
 drones have crushed?
Was there an Urdu Blake whose eyes will never
 open?

Were there some unwritten dervish poems thermobarically
burned?
A Farsi Wordsworth, who'd have praised
Badakhshan's lapis lazuli — the stone which can bring
tranquility to chaos,
The Madonna-blue stone flecked with gold; once
Powdered for pigment, so painters could indicate a
gateway to heaven?

To the Navaho, a young man entering adulthood is
always visited
By a fly while he's in isolation in the desert.
'Big Fly' whispers answers to questions about the
natural order
Which the youth will be asked on returning to the tribe.

But despite another fly's complex circuitry sustaining
bio-diversity,
And being of an intricacy to confound Silicon Valley,
It was judged to have had no place in the television
schedule of a politician,
Who impatiently blew its fuses then looked around
for applause.

Unlike a fly, the White House is unable to change
direction —
Its carbon boot-print firmly indents the planet's neck
As if 'God-given' exceptionalism could guarantee America
Some privileged exemption from the end of civilization.

'It is a mistake of arrogance to mistake size for
significance,'
The *Hellstrom Chronicles* once declared;
But, according to successive Presidents of the
United States,
What's small can't be beautiful, just despised.

'If all the insects disappeared from the earth,'
Jonas Salk has said,
'Within fifty years life would end... whereas,
'If all human beings disappeared from the earth,
'Within fifty years all forms of life would flourish.'

'We should judge every scrap of biodiversity
'As priceless,' E.O. Wilson confirmed;
For, 'If insects were to vanish, the environment
Would quickly collapse into chaos.'

A chaos presided over by a powerless superman who
triumphed over a fly,

Only to find himself ensnared in the darker reaches
of the state, and for he himself to fall —
From being the most popular man in the world to
one of the most culpable —
A fly who made himself the prisoner of an Imperial
web.

Hollywoodland

'I can't talk about Hollywood. It was a horror to me when I was there and it's a horror to look back on. When I got away from it I couldn't even refer to the place by name. "Out there" I called it.'

– Dorothy Parker

'Hollywood is a place that attracts people with massive holes in their souls.'

– Julia Phillips[xiv]

Once upon a time Indian lands were stolen and renamed
'Hollywoodland',
Though for ten thousand years this particular stretch of
soil
Had been the territory of the Chumash tribe, an American
First Nation
Who knew the land by their own name, *Kii-Tovar*, or
'homeland'.

After death-dealing land-grabs by colonists lasting
four centuries,
There were just a thousand Chumash in *Kii-Tovar* in 1900,
When all were evicted by force and their land squared
off in lots,
With a promotional sign erected; it read *Hollywoodland.*

The developers' advertisement had fifty-foot high capital
letters,
Illuminated so they could be seen from miles around.
The developers aimed to sell the land for twenty times
more
Than they'd borrowed, to exploit their high-handed
theft.

Each of the lots on offer was described as an
'upscale location'
And the remaining Chumash chased off for lowering the
tone.
More entrepreneurs were attracted, finding landscape and
climate
Conducive to tale-telling and creating cultural myths.

The citrus fruit now grown on the Chumash's former
territory
Would taste bitter to *Kii-Tovar's* hunter-gatherer tribe.
The ancestral visions of Chumash shamen were now
replaced
By the black-and-white flicker of a mechanical lantern.

Thomas Edison had made 'an instrument which does
for the eye
'What the phonograph does for the ear'.

Designed, in Edison's words, for 'the recording and
reproduction
Of things in motion...' and he'd patented it.

But to save their having to pay royalties on Edison's
patents,
On his machinery and on his film stock,
The new cowboys of celluloid surreptitiously moved
to the west
To be just out of reach of Edison's lawyers.

In 1914 the first feature to be filmed in Hollywoodland
(Soon abbreviated to simply 'Hollywood')
Was called *The Squaw Man*, then renamed
The White Man.
It would anticipate the stories Hollywood liked to tell.

In this melodrama a man comes to the US fleeing a
murder charge.
Saved by an Indian girl called Red Wing, he proposes
marriage.
Later, in the clear, he deserts her on his coming into
an inheritance,
Cruelly indicating that she's unworthy to be a
white man's bride.

The moral implied is that a man may use his fellows
with impunity,
Once he adopts misguided notions of his own
superiority –
As such views were acceptable to the American Empire's
'intelligentsia',
They were uncritically absorbed by the Hollywood
mindset.

To Mark Twain, the author of *Huckleberry Finn*, the
Native American
Was 'ignoble, base, treacherous, and hateful...
'His heart is a cesspool of falsehood, of treachery,
'And of low and devilish instincts.'

In Tom Sawyer, Injun Joe acts out of more than just an
evil nature —
'He is evil,' Twain declares, because of his
'Indian blood.'
Likewise, after the Battle of Wounded Knee —
a prototype for future genocide —
L. Frank Baum, the author of *The Wizard of Oz*,
chillingly declared

That he advocated the total extermination of the Lakota
people.
Since 'the Whites,' he wrote in the *Dakota Pioneer*,

'Are masters of the American continent as they rule
'By law of conquest, and by justice of civilization.'

The 'best safety of the frontier settlements,' he continued,
'Will be secured by the total annihilation of the few
remaining Indians.'
Later, in *The Wizard of Oz,* Baum reaffirmed such
thoughts,
The 'Awgwas' being his hated Indians, thinly disguised,

'You are a transient race,' accused Baum, 'passing from
life into nothingness.
'We, who live forever, pity but despise you...,'
and he'd rejoice in their demise:
'All that remained of the wicked Awgwas was a great
number of earthen hillocks dotting the plain.'
Baum's description deriving from photos of
Wounded Knee's burial ground.

Oz's Yellow Brick Road echoed another crime against
the First Nations,
It was their yellow gold, from their Black Hills that
created the USA
With its road of golden bricks that ran from the Indian
lands in Dakota
To fill Fort Knox and Wall Street and to finance a racist
Hollywood

Whose Westerns were show-reels promoting guns
to kill Indians;
For Indian characters were always 'varmints', as
Doris Day sang,
Although, ironically, Indians were routinely rejected for
Indian film parts
Since it was decided that they didn't look 'Indian' enough.

Then Hollywood's self-mythologizing would serve a new
gold standard
With its racism morphing into nationalism:
'USA! USA!'
And its 'redemption through violence' proved a
strategic ploy
Since inducing fear is essential to the imperializing dream.

Now Hollywood hobbyists and groupies can grade actors
they admire
By their body counts, their 'kills per film', and one year,
in 2010,
Hollywood's fans would count 23,198,862,496 deaths
in 650 films —
Twenty-thousand million bodies to glorify American
exceptionalism.

In Hollywood's eyes, the baddest of 'bad guys' are those
threatening
To subvert 'The All-American Way of Life'.
If they refuse to be slaves to a warmongering corpocracy
Then the 'un-American' deserve to die.

According to *The Los Angeles Times,* when the US
Invaded and occupied Afghanistan after 9/11,
The first buildings they opened in the country they'd
devastated
Weren't hospitals, or clinics, or schools...

But movie theatres — playing American films;
Films that would offer escapist fun and sentimental
endings,
And redemption through violence, and death to all the
bad guys –
Movies that declared, 'Hollywood's the capital of the
planet!'

Hollywood's the place where the display behaviour
of an Empire
Can get sugar-coated by Hollywood's happyendification;
Where Hamlets, Romeos and Juliets have their tragedies
rewritten
And live behind white picket fences in an LA paradise.

In Hollywood, 'If the ending ain't happy, it hasn't
ended yet.'
Issue-based films are only ever made for prestige,
For the studios prefer their moral climate to be
unchanging,
Ensuring that what makes money is their core value.

Anti-war films which aren't a pretext for 'pigging-out'
on violence
Always prove beyond Hollywood's capabilities —
For the Pentagon's in Hollywood to interface with all
war films:
It has script approval so that the Empire looks good.

'Washington and Hollywood spring from the same DNA,'
A Hollywood head honcho, Jack Valenti, revealed;
And Hollywood serves the Empire by making death sexy
And having the morals of someone selling syphilis.

For to run a successful Empire — one with a deadly
reach,
Hell-bent on robbing the world of its resources —
It's handy to lure people into dark rooms and
get them used
To watching people dying in large numbers.

Yet Hollywood mustn't be mentioned without surges of
violins
And without lavish sprinklings of glittering stardust
As it pushes its image, and its branded charisma –
Hollywood!
Burying those whose hopes it has raised and has crushed.

In a Hollywood church, in this empty Shangri-La,
a preacher boasts,
'The entire world gets its entertainment by watching
American films.
'They may not have food,' he yells, 'but they'll sure
watch our films!
'This is our greatest tool to reach the world
for Jesus Christ.'

Outside the church, an anorexic hopeful with dark glasses
Prays she'll be spotted by the celebrity spotters
Whose job's to spot celebrities spotting more celebrities
And, yearningly, she looks up at the Hollywood sign —

The Hollywood sign, where once a girl called
Peg Entwhistle —
Who'd been on Broadway in a play called
The Mad Hopes
And in a murder mystery movie, *Thirteen Women*,
From which her part was cut, and binned —

'Peg Entwhistle, the Ghost of Hollywood'.

Daily News illustration 1932

A rejection she took deeply to heart —
Climbed an abandoned workman's ladder to the top of the
letter 'H'...

There Peg stood with tinsel-town, which had failed her,
spread below,
And its studio commandants making fortunes
from fantasy —
From cowboy porn to war porn, and the pornography
of violence —
Then Peg, aged twenty-four, plummeted down like a
flightless bird.

Peg Entwhistle's body was cremated at
Hollywood Memorial Park,
Now called 'Hollywood Forever', though some might
be tiring
Of a secular death cult with its plutocratic coterie
of screen killers,
In a town named after holly — full of pricks and
drawing blood.

Hollywood's most profitable industry is now porn,
pure and simple —
People trafficked, people commodified, and flesh
pumped

For a sexual anaesthetic, whose value Joseph Goebbels
saw:
He distributed porn in Poland prior to the Nazi
invasion.

Porn's social engineering siphons off all oppositional
threats:
The disaffected can be neutered by the grinding of flesh,
Intellectually undemanding, emotionless, repetitive
and dull;
Endless bodies sprawled on bed sheets, panting for money.

Hollywood now manufactures twelve thousand porn films
a week
Using women who've failed to become *bona fide*
movie stars;
Every year an estimated twenty-five thousand aspiring
actresses
Are sexually exploited by showbiz insiders.

Pornography glues people to screens in an erotic
curfew.
Woe betide the US if it stopped spectating,
And if it started to see the world in a new light
altogether —
Free from the snares of its mass media's war-porn.

In Hollywood movies, almost everyone is svelte, well
groomed, and rich;
Outside, America's homeless shiver impotently in
their tents —
Uncelebrated at Hollywood ceremonies, where a
crimson carpet
Stands in for a century-long smear of
celluloid blood.

Snuff Films at the White House:
The Death of Osama bin Laden

The US President
And his Secretary of State
Are watching snuff films.

US Navy Seals
Line up their chosen victims
Then kill them, one by one.

On a Seal's helmet,
There's a hidden camera
So that images

Of those they're killing
Are fed back by satellite
To a viewing room

Inside the White House
Where the US Navy Seals'
Performance is judged

By the President.
Sheikh Osama bin Laden
Topples. Blood squirting.
The Administration

Watches intently. Savouring
This death-orgasm –

This buzz the powerful
Get when causing death, claiming
That they're still human.

When the audience
Has had its fun, the body
Is dropped into the sea.

Cheers and back-slapping
Follow, 'USA! USA!'
'God loves the USA!'

'The greatest country
'In the history of the world!
'High fives all around.'

The US Emperor can't stop himself there:
Just as all schoolboys enjoy
Pulling wings off flies,

A lens is focused
To watch trophy death-throes
Of an enemy.
As in ancient Rome,

Where crowds bayed for blood and death,
There's ecstatic applause.

The rule of law's absent:
No one's captured. Or tried.
The victim's unarmed.

'Let's watch someone die!'
The commandoes are equipped
To please a voyeur –

'Kill all his women!'
'Wave to the White House, baby,
'We're filming your last breath!'

'Hate our freedoms, huh?
'Hate our Right to Happiness? –
'We'll jerk off while you croak.'

Mr President

'The presidency doesn't exist to exercise power, it disguises power.'
– Anon

'I serve as a blank screen on which people of vastly different political stripes project their own views.'
– Barack Obama, *The Audacity of Hope*

When Richard Nixon
Was the US President,
He told analysts

Of feelings of dread:
'When I look in the mirror,
I see no one there.'

Brought up Christian,
He may have thought twice before
Bombing Vietnam –

He must have doubted
His right to decide whether
To end people's lives.

For, if God exists,
How could you dare to play God?

It would drive you mad.

You'd wake up sweating...
'I ordered the Pentagon
'To fire those missiles;

'I napalmed bodies;
'I can see white phosphorus
'Burning holes in flesh;

'We thought that using
'Depleted uranium
'Was a good idea,

'To harden the shells
'And make them much heavier
'So they'd penetrate;

'I've seen the pictures;
'There are children with two heads;
'They're in my mirror!

'What are they doing...?'
'Are you talking to yourself
'Mr President?'

Another President is caught

In the late watches of the night
Going through the same ritual:

‘I ordered those drones
‘And thermobaric missiles
‘That incinerate

‘People in their homes;
‘Our crews shout “Crispy Critters”
‘And burst out laughing.

‘The Kill Teams I sent
‘In droves to Afghanistan –
‘They kill kids for sport.

‘By doubling budgets,
‘I paid for all their bullets
‘And their cameras

‘So US marines
‘Can shoot passers-by for fun
‘And then play clips back

‘And post them online.
‘Victim’s relatives see them
‘And I see them too.

‘As my soldiers shout
“Got it on camera!” I’m their
‘Commander-in-Chief.

‘3rd platoon soldiers
‘Throw candy out of Stryker
‘Vehicles, drive through

‘Villages, shoot kids
‘Who run out to pick up sweets —
“We love Amriki!” —

‘Smiling at soldiers
‘Who then shoot them. Sweets and blood.
“Amriki, Am...” Bang!

‘Can you imagine?
‘I can’t believe I did it.
‘But the old me’s gone –

‘It’s not in the mirror.
‘All of this must go away.
‘I want me back please.

‘Look, I want me back.
‘Bring my old self back, right now.
‘I’m the President...’

'I'm in the mirror.
'I'm a very good person.
'I'm the President.

'I can do no wrong.'
But cognitive dissonance
And affectlessness

Take a heavy toll
On the man and his image
And they disappear.

For that 'elect me' smile
Will morph into a fixed grin
Ignoring torture

And carnage, sponsored
By a thousand US bases
Promoting Empire –

Bombarding Iraq,
Then Afghanistan, Yemen,
Somalia, Libya...

I'm the President who sells weapons,
In exchange for resources,
To inhuman despots

Enabling them
To loot their own countries and to
Murder opponents.

I make the world safe
For hypocrisy, Wall Street
And blood-money madness.

Improbable threats
To the US are detained
Indefinitely,

While kill-lists of US
Citizens are signed off in
The Oval Office.

For a President's job
Is feeding the war machine
While talking of peace...

A bipolar job.
He farms US tax payers
While promising

That by his spending
Almost all their tax dollars
On security;

On the CIA;
On the State Department, and
On Congress;

On the Pentagon;
On subsidized weaponry
And on the President –

That everyone's safe
But the truth is, war's machine
Keeps Wall Street happy.

A black president
Invades Africa and Libyans
Are killed for oil.

The Empire's demands
Outweigh human values.
It pretends they don't.

A bipolar job,
Where you kill for a peace prize;
You attack six countries,

You launch cruise missiles
For 'humanitarian' wars
With B-2 stealth bombs

Then some fighter jets,
F-16s and F-15s.
'We're superhuman!

'Yo! Geronimo!
'Give me a high-five dude and
'We'll raise the roof-beams!'

Keep Guantanamo
For a concentration camp
Because of 'bad guys'.

To have a conscience
Now means you're a terrorist,
Like Chelsea Manning[xv]...

A White House mirror
Shows a former idealist
Now slaughtering non-stop.

He finds as he kills
That language goes flat. He speaks
In dull platitudes.

The power-hungry are doomed to starve –
If they feed only on their reflections
In the mass media;

All Presidents grow
Uneasy in their own skins
As their true selves fall

Into the abyss;
Tumbling and losing control.
Their meaning has gone –

Their thoughts are double-think.
Speech-writers write all their thoughts
For them to read out

From an autocue;
Their brain's on the other line;
They disintegrate.

Their identity's
Just a chain of feedback loops —
A bankers' sock-puppet.

Their show's continuous
Like *Groundhog Day* — atom bombs,
Agent Orange, drones...

And each President
Is interchangeable in terms
Of their body-mountains.

But when you take lives
You take away your own life,
To join the living dead.

So the mirror's empty,
Exposing each President
As a lethal illusion.

The President of the United States Is Really a Tree

A sequoia in the Sierra Nevada is known as 'The President'.
It's a three thousand, two hundred-year-old redwood.
It's two hundred and forty-one feet high, or twenty storeys,
With a billion pine needles that whisper, 'Beat that!'

It was called 'The President' after Warren Harding,
One of the most pointless Presidents ever.
Harding himself admitted, 'I am not fit for this office
'And never should have been here.'

By contrast the arboreal President presides over a forest,
And has grown from a thin sapling to thirty feet round.
Like Louis Armstrong, the President's gone from poor to
rich
Without hurting anything or anyone on its way.

Not one of the White House's serial imposters
can say that.
Instead of sequestering carbon, producing oxygen
And refreshing the air, they deliver stale, wooden
platitudes,
Scarring the world's countries with their body counts.

In three thousand years this President's crushed no
bones,

It's trod upon no one on the way up;
No one was tortured, no one killed, for this tree to ascend
With its effortless, breathtaking nobility.

Every tree's relationship with its fellow trees is communal.
Trees warn each other under insect attack:
With chemical triggers, their collective immunity's
strengthened
Without single trees telling others what to do.

Man's yearning for power and celebrity is rooted in
fascism:
The idea of one person being adored by millions
Appeals to those who have their eyes on the seats of
control.
But no one's heard of fascist trees. It's inconceivable.

The real President is still growing, in amongst its stand of
trees
Known to local rangers as 'The Congress'.
These Congressmen are uncorrupted by corporate
lobbying,
They just soar in uncomplicated lines to the sky.

The real President is president because of its virtue
Not because it's placed there by vested interests;

The fakes are uprooted after four years, or they're
assassinated,
While the real ones live to over three thousand.

In a graph showing the biggest military spenders,
A tall red column represents the United States.
Its six hundred billion dollars a year towers above the
rest.
This is what the fakes spend on their trunk of death.

The real President conducts water along taproots,
Two hundred feet long, up to the tree's top.
The water of life is cleansed and the air is purified
By a tree that's standing up to the Anthropocene age —

The age in which man is creating a global gear-change,
As threatening as the meteor falls of the Jurassic,
And centuries from now fossils found in the White House
Will testify to the follies of the oncoming age —

The fossilised remains of the dead wood that was
pretending
That it was President of the whole world,
Whilst a life-enhancing tree in the Sierra Nevada was
outliving them all
And was airily disdaining America's death wish.

Image: Colin Gibson

'They wou'd not disdain to dig them up again to make
A homely Meal of them after they had been buried.'

Happy Thanksgiving!

'The Americans have established a Thanksgiving Day to celebrate the fact that the Pilgrim Fathers reached America. The English might very well establish another Thanksgiving Day; to celebrate the happy fact that the Pilgrim Fathers left England.'

– G. K. Chesterton, *Sidelights* (1932)

Despite America's pious self-mythologizing,
This megalomaniac Empire began its career
By eating the corpses of those whose country it had been.
The colony was born from cannibal horror.

Upon landing, the Pilgrim Fathers — the settlers'
Special Forces,
Stern religious fundamentalists from Europe —
Ran out of food and, judging the indigenous people to
be 'savages',
Arrogantly spurned their kind offers of help.

Instead, the settlers hunted local game to extinction,
And, having no idea of the proper crops to plant,
Were unprepared for what they'd call the 'starving time'.
In 1609 they faced famine, as well as drought.

They ate their horses, their dogs, their cats and their
mice;
They made stews out of the Mayflower's rats.
Having fished out the rivers, they sought nutrition in
leather,
And in desperation they chewed their own boots.

A settler named George Percy would leave an account
Of the Pilgrim Fathers' life in Jamestown:
'...Notheinge was Spared to mainteyne Lyfe and to doe
'Those things which seame incredible,

'As to digge upp deade corpses outt of graves
'And to eate them. And some have Licked upp the Bloode
'Which hathe fallen from their weake fellowes...'
Percy claimed that these early Americans,

'Could not wait for their fellows to die before drinking
their blood.'
And he recorded that the 'Extremety of hunger'
Forced these pioneer Founding Fathers 'secrettly in the
night
'To cutt downe their deade fellowes

'From off the gallowes and to bury them
'In their hungry Bowelles.'

The US likes to venerate, if not to canonize, its
    Pilgrim Fathers
But this nation was created by zombie cannibals.

Being incompetent at growing any food, the settlers
Viewed all Indians as a source of protein,
And those they killed in conflict didn't stay buried long.
The settler, Captain John Smith, set the scene:

'Nay, so great was our famine, that a Savage we slew,
'And buried, the poore sort tooke him up againe
'And eat him, and so did divers others. One, another
    boyled
'And stewed him with roots and herbs.'

The early American passion for eating Indians was
    widely known:
In a letter to the King of Spain, Don Alonso de Velasco
Describes how they, 'Eat the dead, and when one of the
    natives died fighting,
They dug him up again, two days afterwards,
    to be eaten.'

Again, one Robert Beverley tells how, 'They eat the
    bodies of the Indians
'They had killed; and sometimes also upon a Pinch
'They wou'd not disdain to dig them up again to make

'A homely Meal of them after they had been buried.'

Thanksgiving may have celebrated the picking of their
first pumpkins,
But this would mask the settlers' more sinister harvest:
The murder of millions of Native Americans over three
centuries –
With every one of them reluctant to, 'Be my guest.'

One record claims that the first Thanksgiving was held
to celebrate
Some settlers escaping from the native population –
From some Pequot Indians angered at their burial
sites being robbed
And dead flesh stolen for the Pilgrim Fathers' delectation.

To justify stealing someone else's territory
Those early US spin-doctors would misrepresent the
Indians:
Just as terrorist Empires now label others terrorists,
They claimed the Native Americans were cannibals
themselves.

Nor has the US lost its taste for devouring human flesh:
From its thousand bases worldwide
The Empire has killed thirty million since World War Two,
And gobbled up their resources on the side.

Every year America comes together to celebrate
Its good fortune at Thanksgiving meals.
It eats tons of white flesh smeared with crimson sauce,
Certain that its God blesses how it feels.

Thanks to years of PR, the Pilgrim Fathers belong not to
history,
But to a quasi-religious ideal.
Established in wartime as a national holiday, Thanksgiving
Now spawns a patriotic fervour that's unreal.

'There is one day that is ours,'
Proclaimed an excited O. Henry, author of *The Cisco Kid*,
'Thanksgiving is the one day that is purely American.
'It's America's defining holiday.'

But to less patriotic pundits it's, 'Nothing
'But a toast to genocide[xvi]',
A day for indulgence in American exceptionalism,
And in an overweening national pride.

America eats 45 million turkeys on Thanksgiving
(Its President spares one in a facetious ritual).
Thanksgiving is spent eating, and drinking, and
eating
And the 'gross-out' prompts a modest proposal:

Modern America's callous division between its rich and
its poor
Has left one in seven households 'food insecure'[xvii]...

Were it to honour its own ancient tradition,
It might dig out its dead rich,
And it might cook them,
And then eat them with impunity.

America: How it Works

'What a country calls its vital economic interests are not the things which enable its citizens to live, but the things which enable it to make war.'

– Simone Weil

The business of America is business
And its number one business is war.
Using Hollywood to peddle its values
It turns the world into its whore.

Its craven citizens are unable to say 'boo'
Or else they'd refuse to pay taxes.
So, like their media, they back every war
That turns the world into ashes.

The most dangerous country in world history
Is the United States of America:
For it believes in murder to further the basest of ends
While holding its creation by God was a miracle.

But the only miracle is its guilt-free attitude to the
holocausts
On which America's foundation is made:

The Native American genocide that killed twenty-five
million
Followed by the North Atlantic slave trade.

It's made no reparation for something that caused
The deaths of a hundred million;
A third holocaust took place in South East Asia, and
one day
America's body count could touch a billion.

A moral retard it wages war upon its own people
Keeping two million of its poorest in jail.
Its gun fetish sees thirty shot dead every day
In a rogue state that's now beyond the pale.

When people were asked in a Gallup poll 'Which
country
'Is the greatest threat to peace in the world today?'
The United States proved to be champion by a very long
way –
Top dog, but a mad dog with whom few wished to play.

A plutocratic kleptocracy whose Senate and Congress
Are stuffed to the roof with spoiled millionaires –
Keen for their supposed enemies to be spied on and
killed
While Congressmen clutch sheaves of arms shares.

Congress props up the military industrial complex
And regularly lunches with its lobbyists,
Promoting arms and fossil fuels to poison the world.
If blood money gets America oil – why resist?

To America its homeless are a feckless subspecies;
The poor are evicted from America's Dream,
America's 1400 newspapers support its every war
For war's how fat cats get to lick up the cream.

In a plutocracy the wealthy are always above the law.
Take rich Texan teenager, Ethan Couch:
He killed four pedestrians while drunk driving but his
lawyer
Pleaded 'Affluenza' in Ethan's defence.

'A disease,' he explained, 'that makes you think that
because you're so wealthy
There'll be no consequences, whatever you do.'
Couch was acquitted and, likewise, America's Corporations
Behave with utter oblivion too.

A Wal-mart employee, Jimmy Damour, was killed by a
frenzied stampede
At a Wal-mart sale as its Long Island store opened.
Although Wal-mart makes trillions selling its slave
labour goods

It refused to compensate a life that its negligence
ended.

The wealth gap in America is pre-revolutionary:
Those at the bottom are forced to flat-line
Whilst the one per cent's spike shoots right off the chart
And the mega-rich cackle, 'It's all mine!'

Every day America's schoolchildren swear their allegiance
To an ubiquitous flag and a feeble constitution
To prompt a sick patriotism that belittles the love of
others
And paves the way for American exceptionalism.

'There's class warfare all right,' says the mega billionaire
Warren E. Buffet, 'but it's my class, the rich class
'That's making the war, and we're winning.' — A moral
bankrupt
Whose dollar bills read, 'In Greed We Trust'.

But the quiet voices of common sense sometimes still
surface
Such as, 'We can't feed the poor but we can fund a war.'
Or, 'If we learn to share there will be enough for everyone.'
And in history the quiet voices can often become a roar.

The Atomic Museum

In the National Atomic Museum
At Albuquerque, New Mexico,
You can buy souvenirs of 'Little Boy',
The bomb that demolished Hiroshima,
And of 'Fat Man', named after the bomb
That flattened Nagasaki three days later.
They come from what the Museum
Calls its 'Exclusive Collection':
'Little Boy' earrings in sterling silver
Cost twenty-four dollars a pair;
While 'Fat Man', the counter clerk says,
'Comes in at thirty dollars' as
'More precious metal is used.'

'They're a great seller,' says the museum storekeeper,
Mike Romero, who assures enquirers,
'We don't hold political opinions.
'We only present the facts.

'If you go to a zoo you can buy a stuffed elephant.
'We are the only atomic museum in the US
'So we have to sell related merchandise.
'I don't think it's tasteless. It was before my time
'And it doesn't strike at my heart at all.'
But the fact that the atomic 'facts'

(Namely everything being obliterated
Within a three-mile radius of the bombs)
Don't strike at his heart at all
Evokes DH Lawrence's unforgiving view —
'The essential American soul is hard, isolate, stoic and
a killer.
'It has never yet melted' —
Written when Lawrence was living in New Mexico,
Later to become the bomb's birthplace,
Where a global bully's big stick
Designed to dish out mega-death
Was first tried out at the Alamagordo test range,
Sowing the seeds of an apocalyptically murderous
meltdown —
A mad Empire's bargaining chip in an unwinnable
game.

The 'facts' are also that to vaporise two Japanese cities
And to sneak new, distorted sicknesses into man's DNA
Was the very lowest and most pointless point
In the entire history of humanity on earth:
For the Japanese had been seeking an honourable
surrender,
But US militarists, keen to stretch the war into
World War Three,
Seized the moment to show Russian rivals who was the
Alpha Male

And which of their misguided boffins was the best,
'USA! USA!' –

Bang went 'Little Boy'. Bang went 'Fat Man'. Then their
pandemics of pain
Launched radioactive waves of political paranoia:
Poison clouds, charged with madmen's thoughts of life
on earth being ended,
Hovered over foreign affairs like blood-sucking bats.
In the Cold War the US had bomb-casing arsenals in
twenty-seven countries
With the plutonium charges needed to render them
nuclear
Hidden in twenty-seven embassies and threatening a
hundred holocausts.

The Atomic Museum was established by
Congressional Charter
To indicate the pride the Empire took in its deadly
heritage.
Though, when the UK journalist James Cameron
Witnessed an atomic test on Bikini Atoll —
Which would turn the surrounding seas into a desert
(Now lovingly commemorated in the Museum
With 'Authentic bomb blast goggles, as used in the
Pacific
'During nuclear testing' being available for purchase) —

Cameron said he thought he could hear a door slam in
Hell.

The Museum's entrance is guarded by phalanxes of
missiles
Pointing, like admonitory fingers: 'Be afraid.
Be very afraid.'
Four California girls drift round the museum's
Heritage Park.
They paw at the bombs, and stroke the undercarriage
of a B-29
Then emerge, giggling, from a mocked-up atomic
shelter
To enter an area set aside by the Museum for more
'Fun Stuff'.
And sprawl over its showcases sizing up the goods on
offer.

There's a 'Fat Man' shot glass, and a 'Little Boy' bottle
stopper;
Posters of mushroom clouds with palm-trees in the
foreground;
Knick-knacks decorated with bombers and their waving
crews;
Reprints of the Daily News, 'ATOM BOMB ROCKS
JAPS'.

There's a 'Get a Half-Life' mug for your favourite
beverage;
Atomic hatpins; atomic tie-clips and nuclear golf balls.
The Museum once even had a line in Atomic Bomb
perfume
Which presumably didn't smell like the end of the
world.

The laid-back visitors spot the Atomic Museum's
jewellery —
Miniature versions of the huge bombs they just strolled
past,
Lying around the Heritage Park like bloated
gravestones.
'Hey, guys. Cute!' One says, poring over the showcases,
'Yeah, gotta have them, dude; you think they come in
gold?'
'What about platinum? Platinum would be dead cool.'

For a split second, the word sounds like 'plutonium' –
'Plutonium would be dead cool', one appears to have
said.
Unfazed, with a numb, laconic smile, as if embodying
death itself,
The clerk slides the triumphalist trophies and trinkets
Across the counter to satisfy their short attention
spans.

'Miss Atomic Bomb'. Las Vegas News Bureau 1947

All four then sidle out of the shop in the Atomic
Museum,
With their bang bang bling now dangling from their
ears.

It's hard not to imagine Cameron hearing another door
slam in this obscene hell
As if, returning from one more mission to make
fear-mongering fun,
The devil has now resurfaced, perhaps to polish his
Zyklon-B paperweight;
Or to buff up his 'Arbeit Macht Frei' keyrings; or to
gloat over Death's Head kitsch
And to tweak his software upgrade of Nazi Playstation 3.

How he cackles, recalling Mary Meyer, the Washington
hostess
Who'd turned Kennedy onto marijuana and to
coke-fuelled sex,
And who'd joked with him in a White House bedroom
About his being high when about to press the nuclear
button.

So then the devil picks out a roach-end, a condom and
a rolled-up bill
And covers them in gold-leaf before giving them pride of
place

In one of the gleaming showcases of the
Atomic Museum,
Amongst the other imperial souvenirs of nuclear folly.

Septimus Severus

From Ancient Rome to Barbarica:
One step forward, two steps backward.

'I've been everything
'And what's the use?'
'*Omnia fui, nihil expedit.*'
Said Septimus Severus,
Invader of Caledonia,
Rebuilder of Hadrian's Wall,
Caesar, and Roman Emperor.

Few modern leaders
Achieve such self-awareness,
Choosing self-delusion
Or self-importance instead.

'Americans buy war like children gobble candy,'
    said Henry Kissinger;
And the Presidential winner
Of the Nobel Peace Prize –
A drone-wielding invader
Of no less than seven countries –
spent a trillion dollars
On refurbishing his nuclear arsenal[xviii].

Although the American Emperor's fame has gone viral
His name is surely no longer worth mentioning
For, instead of his despairing of himself,
He preferred having the world despair of a man
Who treacherously used his Imperial power
To steal the world's tomorrows.

His fame may become fissile in form
With every man, woman and child
On the planet treated to a particle
Of his weapons' grade plutonium.

Elected on an anti-war platform
He campaigned for a 'nuclear-free world'
Only to be leaving in his wake
An unstable trail
Of radioactive dust.

The Dying Bee

'The state represents violence in a concentrated and organized form. The individual has a soul, but as the state is a soulless machine, it can never be weaned from violence to which it owes its very existence.'

— Mahatma Mohandas K. Gandhi

Weapons are the United States premier export
So the right marketing strategy is called for,
And that strategy for its number one product-line
Is war – mindless and endless American war.

It turns out that in Bush's build-up to Iraq,
All the so-called 'reasons' were irrelevant:
The US and the Pentagon were hell-bent on war
And nothing would put them off the scent.

While more than half of every US tax dollar
Which its citizens pay to their government
Goes to the US's military-industrial complex,
US citizens comply with such arrangements.

The sole escape for a captive, warmongering citizenry
Is to make war upon their own country:
A tough call since the US is a police state
And its democracy's really a plutocracy –

Whose rash spending of six trillion dollars on war
Over the last four years,
Whilst 1.6 million are homeless and 16 million
undernourished
Displays a dangerous poverty of ideas.

Their country was once founded upon an idea
But US ‘freedom’ now has a hollow ring:
It’s as free as a dying bee with misplaced pride
In its unlovely and redundant sting.

For the last thirty years, sixty percent
Of the US’s national income
Has gone into the pockets of its richest one percent;
Only to be passed onto its privileged children –

Rich kids who jeer at those less fortunate
On their twittering social media,
Betraying passive-aggressive desires to kill them all off
As they record their feelings of hateful hysteria.

‘How are you white and homeless?’ one whines,
‘What a waste of life and opportunity.’
‘I wonder if homeless people go to heaven.
‘I hate the homeless,’ they add with crass insensitivity.

‘I don’t feel sorry for them. If you want change
‘Then let me throw it as hard as I can at your dirty
face.’
‘I hate when it gets cold out,’ another tweets,
‘Cuz then all the homeless people get on the bus.’

‘I did my good deed today,’ chimes a third,
‘I gave some worthless bum a quarter at the mall.’
‘I was enjoying a latte when I almost vomited.
‘Across the street, I saw a hobo girl.’

‘Get back to your side of the bridge. No one likes you.
‘That’s what I wanted to say.’
‘A bum tried fighting me last night cus I told him
to get a job haha’
‘In all honesty, I kinda don’t feel bad for homeless
people.
‘Each individual is in control of their life
‘And future, so it’s all their fault.’

Another vouchsafes, ‘If homeless people
‘Don’t want to freeze to death,
‘Why don’t they just find homes?!
‘I mean DUUUUHHHHHH.’

'Never understood why homeless people smell of piss
'When you can literally piss anywhere.'
'I hate when homeless people expect us to feel sorry for
them
'We all have the same 24 hrs.
'What you chose to do with it is up to you.'

'If home is where the heart is, then are homeless people
heartless?'
'All homeless bums are loser drug addict drunks.'
'Maybe if homeless people took care of themselves,
'Maybe if they looked pretty,
'We would want to help them more
'But I don't help yellow teeth.[xix]'

In a country so devoid of a social conscience
Alien objects are ready to fill the vacuum:
Money; guns; dead food; a fetishized military —
All bypass the need for compassion.

In the US the police arrest people for feeding the
homeless
And as a result many homeless have died –
They've also been used for random target practice
Revealing the heartless nature of the divide.

It’s a country with a neurotic death wish
Whose police kill a thousand a year;
Its mass media peddle the self-promotions
Of an armed pornocracy living in fear.

If that’s not a pre-revolutionary situation
Then it’s hard to know what is one:
Its rich taunt the poor with their limitless wealth;
The poor are sickened by their destitution.

Meanwhile the pollinating honey bee is dying;
Killed off by the greediest nation in history –
Bludgeoning soil with chemical hammers to speed
growth
And polluting air to fog the bees’ trajectory.

Name a Radical Film

'Where any view of Money exists, Art cannot be carried on, but War only'

— William Blake

'I so hate the rich. I really cannot bear their company... but to raise dosh [to make films] I would have to court the rich.'

— John Berger on why he decided not to pursue a career in filmmaking

Name a radical
Film. And now name another.
Now name a few more.
You can't name many
Because there are very few.

Films cost a fortune
And to produce them
You have to spend time with rich
People with money.
They aren't radical,
On the whole. That's why they're rich.

So, you eat their food,
You gulp down their drinks,

Laugh at their jokes then maybe
Get driven about
In plush SUVs.
Fly to Cannes in their Lear Jets
Then laugh at their jokes.
Again and again.
'I didn't tell you that one
Before?' 'Oh, no. No...'

'Right. Shoot. Let's hear it.
Give me the log-line. The pitch.
One sentence will do.'
The attention span
Of the rich is very short.
They have distractions.
A radical film
Might be an amusing thought
But they'll draw the line
At paying for
Their world to be destroyed.

Hollywood's algae,
That clouds the human psyche
And exudes a poisonous gas
Is spawned by tainted cash:
Money that's laundered
From stocks and shares

In Third World Labour
By beady-eyed gamblers
On commodities;
In other words, on people's food.

Then bloated by profits
From oil and from arms
The rich think that it might be fun
To sink millions into films:
To buy some glamour,
To acquire some reflected stardust
To sprinkle on their trophy wives.

Why do films portray
The lives of the privileged
Disporting their wealth,
Looking alluring,
Physically immaculate,
All bought by money?
Why are criminals
So romanticized in films –
Bonnie and Clyde, and Capone?
Because they're screen projections
Of the feral rich who are
Backing the business.

'Let's see the money
On the screen,' industry
Bosses boorishly demand,
'*Plus lots of weapons...'*
For film bloodbaths
Are PR for the arms trade —
For the MIC, the Military
Industrial Complex.
Which has fingers in every pie,
And he who pays the piper
Calls a profitable tune –
A tune whose repetitious hook-line
Drips blood in perfect time:
'So let's please see lashings
Of bone-crushing, flesh-tearing
State-of-the-art long-distance
Thermobaric splatter-guns
And lots of them. Repeat.
Lots and lots and lots of them.
If it bleeds, it leads!' – Just as
In the newspaper business,
War always trumps peace
And no anti-war film
Gets made unless it can provide
The juiciest gore-fest.

Films serve the system.

Watch the extras on a set,

They're treated like slaves.

Those in the business

Speak in hushed tones of 'players' —

Influential elites,

Hard-nosed bean-counters

Who may 'play' but aren't much fun,

As their antennae

Are tuned to wealth, and

To snorting up the souls

Of those they can exploit

In La La Land's Californian HQ

Where goodness is no good.

'Okay, so what's your pitch –

'The love lives of the homeless

'Shot in some tent city?

'Who's gonna watch that...?

'And who are you gonna go to

'For backing? Campesinos?

'Peasant farmers? Janitors?

'Maybe my Mexican gardener?

'Or my Filipino housemaid?

'Or my Puerto Rican driver?

'Or my Haitian bodyguard?

'Maybe ***they'll*** *all back you?*

'Get lost you limey schmuck.'

The stifling algae blooms and
Epiphany fades...
Time spent with the rich
Always means losing your edge,
Somehow or other.

When the Lumière
Brothers produced their first films
In 1895
'La Poste' in Paris
Foresaw that, *'When this device*
'Is available
'To the French public
'Everyone will be able
'To photograph those
'Who are dear to them.
'Not just in their immobile
'Form but also in
'Their movements, and with
'Speech on their lips. Then death
'Will no longer be absolute.'

The very first films of all
Were instantaneously
Latched onto by people

As being something hopeful –
A way of dealing with pain
By assuaging grief
And bettering things.

Instead, millions have been killed
For cinema's spectator sport
And those in the dark
Like mushrooms, quietly curfewed,
Watch death after death
Whilst La La Land's territorial,
Egomaniac and bully-boy values
Are judged to be sacrosanct:
'That's mine! I'm armed.'
'This woman is mine.'
'We're tooled up and dangerous!'
'You are history.'
'Give me the money.'
'Get your sorry ass out of here.'
'You're dead meat.'

Vicious and vengeful scenarios
Devised by dysfunctional nerds
Whom no one would play with at school.

Try to quote any dialogue
That says, 'Why don't we share this?'

It's not how the system works.

Name a radical film
That anaesthetizes war,
Sends money packing,
Has real trees growing
Out of the cinema screen
Bearing tasty fruit
So audiences strip
And become possessed by Pan
Then turn into fauns
Leap into the air...

No, they slink out, glazed and drained,
Blinking like mole rats,
Then shake the dust off their feet,
As if the cinema they've just attended
Has sick building syndrome.

What if screens were to vanish?
Everyone would still
See what needed to be done
Without the media
Mediating stuff
Twenty-four frames a second —
Or digitally mincing it all up
Into baby food —

Digestible images
That can usurp life
So that people feel like
They've done something
If they've just watched
A film about something...

When Lee Harvey Oswald
Shot Kennedy he escaped
From reality
To a movie-house...
He hid in a cinema
To feel more unreal.

The Lion and the Lamb

The Metro Goldwyn Mayer lion was persuaded to roar
Then its head was surrounded by a frame
Reading 'MGM Trade Mark' as it was suborned into
serving
Hollywood's moneyed cult of fame.

It roars to further the reach of the American Empire.
It's there as the Land of the Free's sad captive.
Its repetitive abuse serves the Empire's soft power
Whose magic in close-up isn't attractive.

There are only twenty thousand lions left alive
Throughout the entire African continent.
Rich American trophy hunters pay to shoot them
Then film themselves looking triumphant.

But when nature's wildness is anaesthetized
And when its stars are decapitated for sport
Then the transmigration of souls may dictate
That man's most bestial dragons run riot.

Innocent skies now hide diabolical drones
Randomly targeting those below –
Incinerating them with thermobaric bombs
To snuff out life's luminous glow.

If there are no more wild Kings of the Jungle,
If mechanized man is now the great 'I am' –
True visions of peace and paradise will evaporate
There being no lion to lie down with the lamb.

The President of the United States is Weeping

The President of the United States is weeping:
He's welling up at the news of the death
Of elementary school kids and college students
Due to callous killers stealing their breath.

Since Sandy Hook in Connecticut in 2012,
When twenty children were shot dead,
There've been seventy-four school shootings
Yet the writing on the wall stays unread.

To the President such events are inexplicable:
'How could anyone do such a thing?'
Dim Presidents can cause extreme damage
When the right bells in their brains don't ring.

Last year, the President was number one —
Number one weapons dealer in the world —
To sign off thirty-six billion dollars of arms sales
It's essential that your heart be stone cold;

And that your head remain quite oblivious
To your weapons going astray:
For missiles and Humvees end up with ISIS –
Only to attack you one day.

Likewise the kudos and the cash you derive
From your having a militarised mind
Come at a heavy price thanks to *karma*'s law
Which can bite you hard on the behind.

Your own children can die like the victims
Of those to whom you peddle your toys.
Yet you ensure the income derived from arms
Stifles any and every dissenting noise.

Anyone pointing to the dangers of blowback
Is roundly dismissed as a crank;
Blowback's ignored because the cries of children
Aren't able to put money in the bank.

While the President makes a show of weeping
For Sandy Hook Elementary School,
Links between this and the arms trade are clear
To anyone save an all-American fool.

The President is the high priest of a gun cult
Which spawns thousands of devotees
Who shoot thirty thousand a year stone dead
And bring his own country to its knees.

The US arms trade exposes the hypocrisy
Of the President's crocodile tears

For body counts are trumped by share prices
And fear-mongering profiteers –

Profiteers who hire powerful lobbyists
To visit the White House in droves
And ensure that half the world's arms sales
Are of the weapons the US so loves.

The US War Machine's annual budget could buy
Each homeless American a million dollar home –
If the imperial government were ruled by compassion
Instead of a murderous suicide syndrome.

295 857

The Dalai Lama, ISIS and America

The Dalai Lama has said that America created ISIS
Through its use of drones and its waterboard torture,
For the US has exempted itself from the rule of law
And become no more than an international butcher.

Tibetan Buddhism's spiritual leader urged the
Administration
'To alter America's catastrophic foreign policies.'
He was in Moscow at the Bolshoi Theatre, where he was
inaugurating
A festival: 'Tibet: Traditions, Art, Philosophy and Peace'.

He chastised the President for supporting fallacious
Saudi clerics
Who claim to represent Islam by siding with cut-throats:
'Thus they give the radical groups an excuse
for their crimes',
Those who heinously murder the innocent, and
then gloat.

'Several times I importuned President Obama,'
He said, as he outlined his geopolitical fears,
'To end his catastrophic support for Saudis and their
terrorist proxies
'In the Middle East, but my appeals fell on deaf ears.'

Presidents have been happily photographed
bowing to the Saudi King,
For their economy depends on Saudi oil's
poisonous spouting.
Like every prostitute politician each President claims
to have vision
As they cravenly capitulate to Wall Street's touting.

In ISIS's latest propaganda video — as Saudi oil spurts
Into the gas tanks of American automobiles —
A Yemeni is escorted into the desert by chanting captors.
His eyes and his mouth show the terror he feels.

In Arabic, the lead captor explains to the camera
That 'the enemy must be crushed',
Then he bends down to pick up a boulder
And the Yemeni man's head is smashed.

His eyes are closed in agony as the boulder's removed.
Gouts of blood jet from his distorted mouth.
The ISIS participants film their victim's last seconds
As his bloodstained eyes open in terrified disbelief.

The boulder's picked up, then it's dropped.
The event is chronicled by ISIS's Cyber Army.
A remorseless, triumphal chant is added as soundtrack:
'The soldiers of Allah are ready'.

In the White House's Oval Office the President of
Barbarica
Signs his Wednesday 'kill list' with a golden pen
And the enemies of the Imperium are duly dispatched
Through State assassination or a robot drone.

The flow of the President's pen leads directly
To crimson stains in Yemen's distant dunes,
But Imperial power is impervious to reason
And the White House can't read the runes.

In political science as well as in physics
Every action that anybody takes
Has an equal and opposite reaction, like *karma*:
A drop of blood shed can grow into lakes.

NOTES

---

[i] American writer, William S Burroughs once worked as a pest controller, an experience he recounted in his novel *Exterminator*.

[ii] Property magnate Fred Trump was once arrested at a Klu Klux Klan (KKK) rally and was sued, in 1973, by the Justice Department for refusing to rent his flats to black people. https://www.vice.com/en_us/article/all-the-evidence-we-could-find-about-fred-trumps-alleged-involvement-with-the-kkk

[iii] Nick Penzenstadler, and Susan Page, 'Trump's 3,500 lawsuits unprecedented for a presidential nominee', *USA TODAY*, 2 June, 2016

[iv] Trump accused of 'savage sexual attack' on a 13-year-old girl, http://www.news.com.au/finance/work/leaders/donald-trump-accused-of-savage-sexual-attack-on-a-13yearold-girl/news-story/6585a49357159ff2fdc3ff3933370500 July 5, 2016. Lisa Bloom, Attorney and legal analyst for NBC News and Avvo, 'Why The New Child Rape Case Filed Against Donald Trump Should Not Be Ignored' *Huffington Post,* 29th June, 2016; updated, July 1st, 2016

[v] Brad Hoff, 'Hillary Emails Reveal True Motive for Libya Intervention: Newly disclosed emails show that Libya's plan to create a gold-backed currency to compete with the euro and dollar was a motive for NATO's intervention.' *Foreign Policy Journal,* January 6, 2016

[vi] The Islamic State of Iraq and Syria (also referred to as ISIL and *Daesh*) an Islamist entity directly descended from *al-Qaeda* — itself, arguably, the result of the West's interventions in Afghanistan and Iraq.

[vii] http://dailycaller.com/2016/09/16/just-5-7-percent-of-clinton-foundation-budget-actually-went-to-charity/

[viii] CNBC, 26 Sep 2016

[ix] John R. O'Donnell, James Rutherford, *Trumped! The Inside Story of the Real Donald Trump--His Cunning Rise and Spectacular Fall*, Simon & Schuster, 1991

[x] Nick Paumgarten, The Death and Life of Atlantic City, *The New Yorker*, September 7, 2015

[xi] Tom McCarthy, 'Donald Trump reverses position on torture', *The Guardian,* 4 March 2016

[xii] To Trump: "the concept of global warming was created by and for the Chinese in order to make U.S. manufacturing non-competitive."

[xiii] CNBC is an American cable television broadcaster, part of NBC Universal news group

[xiv] Author of *You'll Never Eat Lunch in This Town Again.*

[xv] Born Bradley Edward Manning, Chelsea is a trans woman who was sentenced in 2013 to 35 years in prison for providing

Wikileaks with three-quarters of a million military and diplomatic documents in 2010. The leaked material, particularly the diplomatic cables, was seen by some commentators as a catalyst for the Arab Spring. Manning also exposed a video which showed two American helicopters firing on a group of ten men in Baghdad, two of whom were Reuters employees. The US Pilots mistook their cameras for weapons, and expressed notable glee at their shooting. This leaked footage caused a sea-change in public opinion about the war.

[xvi] Steven Evans

[xvii] http://www.povertyusa.org/

[xviii] 'US begins $1 trillion upgrade of Nuclear Weapons Arsenal.' International Business Times, November, 15, 2014

[xix] All quotes are from actual tweets.